PERIPHERAL VISION

PERIPHERAL VISION

MARTIN DOLAN

Peripheral Vision
Recent Work Press
Canberra, Australia

Copyright © Martin Dolan, 2018

ISBN: 9780995353893 (paperback)

 A catalogue record for this book is available from the National Library of Australia

All rights reserved. This book is copyright. Except for private study, research, criticism or reviews as permitted under the Copyright Act, no part of this book may be reproduced, stored in a retrieval system, or transmitted in any form by any means without prior written permission. Enquiries should be addressed to the publisher.

Cover photograph: © Martin Dolan, 2018
Cover design: Recent Work Press
Set by Silvana Moro

recentworkpress.com

For Cynthia, as always.

Contents

Chaos Theory	1
Without Visa	2
Against Nature Poetry	3
Unless There is Water	4
Hogmanay	5
Coffee Break	6
Aubade	8
Instructions Not Included	9
When Life Fails to Resemble Fiction	10
Déjà Vu	11
Two Sunsets	13
Another Sea	14
Non-Stop	15
Bees Dancing	16
Dung Beetles	17
Pebbles on the Water	18
Dangerous Activity	19
Correspondence	20
Unmentionable	21
Observing Childhood	22
Everything Must Pass	23
As the Flower of Grass	24
In a Dry Year	26
She Washes Him	28
Dust	29
Scenes from a Silent Film	30
Gut Feeling	32
Kafka at Work	33
Official Greetings	34
Plato as World Traveller	35

The Idea of Busan	36
A Guide to Bohemia	38
A Mind of Winter	39
Near the Maelstrom	40
After Returning	41
In the Wilderness	42
The Feast of Valentine	44
Labyrinth	46
No Looking Back	47
A Hundred Times	48
Knock on Wood	49
Afterword	50

Chaos Theory

Sometimes it works the other way:
a cyclone funnels mass drowning
north through the Bay of Bengal;
three days later a butterfly
sipping Tasmanian nectar
is prodded sideways by a breeze.
Eight thousand deaths. One butterfly
nudged sideways by a puff
of southern air.
                    It was like this
forty years ago when we met:
you cool, slim in a pastel dress;
the chance moment of eyes locking;
the unforeseeable result.

Without Visa

This calm is not what I was born into.
Sunny streets do not chime with memory
of misting rain, of dogshit underfoot,
dank smells of cabbage and old cooking fat,
orange sodium lights grating the night.

A walk away, grandmother's grimy flat
on its dingy stairwell has sideslipped
into brightness of skylights and blond wood,
self-importance of coded entry locks,
late-model cars elbowing up the street.

The past does not become a foreign place.
Rather, we who leave it behind have changed
allegiance, have taken up new passports
then are surprised one day, seeking entry
without visa, to be stopped at the border.

Against Nature Poetry

Here in a place of grudging permissions,
of surveyed space doled out like charity,
of windows grimacing at each other
and cold light squeezed from vapour and coatings
where even real plants look artificial,
waxed, immobile in dry unchanging air,
we look for signs in the smallest of things:
how the shadows grow, how a cockroach treks
across a grey waste of carpet to hide.

This morning, as we sat in the sunlight
with all the small pieces of dailiness
a bird threw itself against the window
and fell senseless, twitching. A sparrow's fall.
It stirred, then shrugged and staggered into air.
Later, as I drove here, half-attentive
there was a fox dismembered on the road,
crushed body to the right, head to the left.
All cars drove on, stopping only for lights.

We look for signs in the smallest of things:
a dead bluebottle bursting underfoot
as we walk unshod on an evening beach,
uncertainty about where the first star
might show itself, the pattern of the waves,
a sparrow that did not see fresh-cleaned glass,
a fox crushed and bloody among the wheels,
the careless survival of a cockroach
scurrying off under fluorescent lights.

Unless There is Water

There is nothing to be seen in this stone
nothing to nudge recollection
of why it is here with a dry rosebud
and a green length of creased ribbon.

The ribbon is a cold night dancing drunk
the rosebud an autumn picnic
in a country churchyard where yellow leaves
shivered down slant sunlight to rest.

The stone is nothing until you take it
and drop it in a glass of water
so colours leap out like summer morning
when sunlight shatters on the sea.

There was a night when you drove for hours
to where ocean greyed into dawn
and wet pebbles glittered in sunrise.
Somewhere you have kept a picture.

Hogmanay

Two in the morning and the new year in
with the whisky at its low water mark
we talk above wave thump
and splash, as the white moon
pulls the sea in to the beach.

Four years and half a world separated
our births, my brother and I, and fifty
have brought us to this place
to this understanding
as changeable and constant as the waves.

This one night of the year he was the one:
dark-haired, chosen and thrust into the dark
of a coming midnight
for a welcome return
bearing whisky and coal, shortbread and luck.

Another year will bring what it needs to:
no ritual or propitiation
can match this warm summer,
swing of southern stars
above banksias and waves rolling in.

Coffee Break

> *Seated in silence, clothed in silence*
> *And face to face—the room is small*
> *But thronged with visitants—*
> *We ask for nothing: we have all.*

> Robert Graves Strangeness

A fly freezes to the window pane
as the fan circles. It twitches, leaps
away on invisible curves of air,
sneaks back to sidle across glass
distracting my half-focussed gaze
from soft promises of violence
disguised as strangers' conversation.
Holding a year's anger in a cup
I peer again into summer brilliance
seated in silence, clothed in silence

watching from interior greyness.
Once more I am waiting for you
in this small café with its large view
this always unstable fulcrum
of our tense balance. I hold tight
against a crackling urge to sprawl
in diffractions and reflections
across the heat eddies of summer.
I note instead others by the wall
and face to face—the room is small

small with the clenched intimacies
of a long claustrophobia—
watch two others exchange glances
as secret as their words are low.
They each stand carefully as though
nothing is left but the tolerance
of separate bills and separate
departures into sunlight:
gestures with elegant surfaces
but thronged with visitants

with ghosts of long relationship
as importunate as beggars.
The strangers leave as you arrive
to peer blindly into these shadows
with summer's dazzle in your eyes.
There is one last thing to scrawl
on this page before I wave lightly
to bring us together again
face to face and backs to the wall.
We ask for nothing: we have all.

Aubade

whether we slept
whether my breathing fell in step with yours
whether all night the scent of daphne
whether we found the right words
whether your hair spread out on the pillow
whether we heard the clock ticking
whether you stood naked by the window
whether we needed any words
whether the bed was warm where you had been
whether the birds began singing
whether this dawn or some other
whether you looked back

Instructions Not Included

Each morning drops
in twists and turns of dream,
the slow assembly by rote—
the instructions lost—
of some new thing to meet day
and greetings and smallest talk.

An eyebrow raised in query
ways of standing, embracing
and words placed together
tightened, braced into solidity
but always something behind,
left over.

When Life Fails to Resemble Fiction

The time comes when it's clear there is no story.
Each incident stands alone, gangly, loose-limbed,
glancing casually at its companions,
feigning indifference. Crises come and go
arbitrarily, unplotted, resolving
nothing, not even themselves. Conclusions loom
overt as morning fog and as transient,
melting into the day's ordinary air.
A guessed half-way or so along a rough track
we discover the dark wood is all there is,
traversed by wandering paths, without clear bounds;
there may be a gate, perhaps a waiting guide
but he offers only day trips into hell
then back to where the animals prowl in darkness.

Déjà Vu

So the world happens twice—
once what we see it as,
second it legends itself
deep, the way it is.

William Stafford Bifocal

It begins unnoticed
this sinking through reluctant time
this feathering down
past surreptitious hours and days
as slow as afternoon
until the world is less precise—
chronology has gaps—
through them we can achieve this
languid seeing through former eyes
so the world happens twice.

There is no bottom yet
no guarantee it will be soft
except for a promise
made uncertainly.
We try to weigh its value
against all the things the world says
but in this free falling
nothing has the weight to balance
the past's claim that it was
once what we see it as

falling through this afternoon
falling until we have arrived
at where I was before
when I did not recognise it
back in this room where I know
each single cup upon the shelf
and will know them again.
The round clock ticking on the wall
will replicate each new
second. It legends itself

into another room
that will be exactly the same—
I have been there as well.
Now that I have fallen with you
from that room's certainty
to the unlikelihood of this
which gave it a future
at last we can carefully
replace memory where it lay—
deep, the way it is.

Two Sunsets

A path twists between bent trees
and up. Our shadows waver
long in front of us and blur
as the light softens to red.
Halfway up the reaching slope
we stop, turn to the dazzle
of a fat sun on grey hills,
watch its red fall behind twilight.
No words. Our eyes meet and part.
We turn to the path and run
dodging past the shadowed trees,
dry bark crunching underfoot.
Twigs crackling, breath rough, we run
up to the hilltop boulders,
warm still and lit by the sun.
One sunset is not enough
and now we have a second
as breathing steadies, pulses
syncopate in our joined hands.
When it is gone, the red coin
rattled down the slot to night,
a wind slides up the hill, cold.

Another Sea

This sea is not mine, though bitter
with the same salt, blued by the same sky.
Here a solstice sun lopes the firth;
the day doubles like an echo,
seagulls cross intersecting years.
These cottages, re-tenanted
with incomers, have forgotten
cleared Highlanders reconfigured
as fishermen then moved on again.
An historian's child, I played
here once in a present now past;
returned today, I have nothing
to do except gather pebbles
and skip them across wavelets
to drown.

Non-Stop

Arrived at nowhere he stops,
steps out of his car,
carefully traces the dune
down to shrugs of sea,
sees how randomly the waves
weave foam at his feet,
fitfully reflect a moon
manacled. The sand
sends rumours into the night.
Not looking, clothes piled,
pulls back straight and steps forward
wordless and the foam
fumbles his shins till he falls
full-length and, stroke by stroke,
strikes out for elsewhere, non-stop.

Bees Dancing

By waggle and turn, waggle and turn
of dance on the tesserae of comb
bees trace a shape of infinity
to point out where sweetness lies.

If this is dance there should be music
to guide steps and beats to set their pace
but here is factory, not ballroom;
it hums with work's monotone.

Consider the flowers of the field:
there is nothing there but sustenance
of fluffed pollens and sugared nectars
gathered for the trembling hive;

nectar inhaled, transmuted, spat out
and sucked again, spat again, capped up
with wax into hexagonal cells,
a patient store of honey.

Then winter hunkers on the world, cold
sneaks into walls and crevices and stays
where bees come together to crowd
and shiver their sisters back to warmth.

They will eat what we have left behind,
remnants of their summer's foraging,
will change places, taste and change again,
dancing their lack. They will hum.

Dung Beetles

Sun trundles up the slope of morning
cows slobber their cuds towards milking
a plane chalks a line across the sky
and birds twitch for insects in the grass
where dung sits brown and the beetles work.
In Luxor you can touch for good luck
statues of scarabs, buy amulets
of faience or stone to ward evil.
These beetles belong to the sun god
rolling their brown wheels along the ground.
They are busy in this slow morning
shaping dung into balls, rolling them
through afternoon, evening and the sun's
slow drop into night. The stars come out
and the Milky Way spills its white spray.
Still beetles roll. Sharp eyes read stars,
moonlight, tracking towards morning.

Pebbles on the Water

The way a pebble skips across water,
skitter and bounce and then quick drowning,
reminds him of how, before she turned and left,
she started, stopped and started again to say

(every skitter and bounce and then quick drowning
of words like unwanted kittens in a pool)
she started, stopped and started again to say
she'd had enough of everything, enough

of words like unwanted kittens in a pool,
of feelings that were never complete.
She'd had enough of everything, enough.
He looked back on long days that were empty

of feelings, that were never complete
to her satisfaction or his. He said how
he looked back on long days that were empty
striving after an arrangement of affairs

to her satisfaction or his. He said how
the most that he could do was never enough;
striving after an arrangement of affairs
seemed so much futility and waste of time.

The most that he could do was never enough.
The restless twitching of mynahs in dry grass
seemed so much futility and waste of time.
She took those agitated steps towards him.

The restless twitching of mynahs in dry grass
reminds him of how, before she turned and left,
she took those agitated steps towards him
the way a pebble skips across water.

Dangerous Activity

Irony was cheap in those days:
I could buy a line for thirty dollars;
with a noseful I felt like God
and God was a woman because you were.

I still get the biggest flashbacks
walking through prosy shopping malls;
I feel the rush and swirl as though
a tab of surrealism has taken hold:
the crowds catch fire and melt.

Correspondence

It's hard to remember whether you
stopped sending those long empty letters
first or whether I swore off writing.
I only remember that it ended
slowly, the way a creek dries in drought.
Will you recognise my crabbed scrawl
through years and metamorphosis of print?
Will you care? The worm of feeling
cocooned in my scratchy paragraphs
was invisible to me
mimicking that hollowness from you
that I refused to know. I still see
the space you formed round cursive words.
We wrote against distance. Distance won.

Unmentionable

This is not to be spoken of
but wrapped for storage
put away to gather dust
on a shelf at the back of the mind
a precarious stored thing
that one day falls at your feet
undeniably solid
and demands that you open it.

Observing Childhood

This boy looks like someone else
crouched outside green weatherboard
squinting through rippled light of gums
on this newest edge of town.

He has not yet explored
creeks stabbed by willow saplings
paddocks of impartial cows
has not barbed himself on wire.

The yabbies are still a secret
hidden in undiscovered dams
beyond the raw wooden fence
that blows wind into peering eyes.

Instead he pushes tiny cars
through parched clumps of grass
draws intersecting curves
to map an abandoned city.

A yellow pile of builder's sand
too fine and dry for tunnels
stands for memory of hills
in a country green with distance

sand like faded gorse flowers
not weathered enough to match
dried grass of this day's summer
that flanks the road to nowhere.

Everything Must Pass

> *There is a needle 'I' between the past and the now through which everything must pass.*

Inga Clendinnen Agamemnon's Kiss

See how evening blows through the curtains
and smell the scent of the rose bush
still here through all the neglect.
Remember the cutting that I struck
under your irritated guidance
from the bush my mother had planted.

It is not enough. A scent cannot
draw you back, nor could a trench of blood.
All that is left is the needle eye
through which a thin past can be threaded
if my eye is sharp enough to see
and memory holds my hand steady.

As the Flower of Grass

Mary Dolan (1931-2004)

We drove through the cold week before Easter,
just the two of us, this time, side by side,
the car larger than before, one child absent,
the other making her own arrangements.
Two years' drought had bleached the grass,
had thinned the sheep and shrivelled the dams
by narrow roads not taken since those years
when we paid long-distance service to kin
every second Easter and Christmas.
Further north the summer rain had drawn out
hesitant blades of new grass from red soil
and the trees stood tensely full of water.
Grasshoppers leapt in a flurry and flew
against the windscreen as though to distract
thoughts from her parallel journey, coffined,
alone, towards a gathering family.
No dying at home for her, no fading
into dementia.
Flick! Another grasshopper bounced away
smearing clean glass with its yellow entrails.
Another, another: such endless slaughter
for two hundred kilometres that at last
our car's red was hidden by the yellow
and our vision blocked by a wall of corpses.
We stopped then under grey autumn clouds
to scrub and rinse away the evidence.
The smell remained: the sharp smell of mown grass
carried with us to the door of a house

that was no longer home to her or me;
carried with us to the solemn church,
to the neat rows of the cemetery
where we laid her in red soil under grass
in the yellow light of the angled sun.
All flesh is as grass. The smell is with us still.

In a Dry Year

That country can reach out and squeeze memory
from shrivelled years stored away like autumn fruit,
can push blood faster so ears hear, so eyes see
how the angle of afternoon light surprises
by its sudden breaking out, by how light cuts
the sedulous haze over surrounding hills
to thin folds of red soil and bones of granite
while air shuffles leaves and birds chirp nervously.

You must work to find horizons there, must climb
bald tors to see faded sky meet earth cleanly
and even then wind-whipped eyes can blur.
Secrets grow in cherry and apple orchards,
among black beef cattle huddled under trees,
hide themselves like cells twisted wrong by sunlight
waiting their chance. This year, next year can slide past,
lives can drift and scatter while cells grow, divide.

We gained our share of these tablelands cheaply:
fifty years, three graves, a scatter of ashes
to buy space for our stories to put down roots;
we left them there and went looking for new things.
We still pay a price and paying brought us back
to huddle, to grieve, to resurrect old jokes
and make new ones, cracking hardy though we knew
this was a dry year, the auspices were bad.

Sibling-strangers, we gathered around a death
and—crude accounting of life—around a birth,
uncertain how a new balance would be found.
We tried stilted conversation, lumbering

through steps of a dance we were still to learn;
tried rituals of grief, tried words, tried music
to meet unwritten rules of expectation;
tried drunken confidences on a cold night.

That country can reach out and squeeze memory
into something new, but it waits to be asked.
We drove our slow convoy over gravel roads,
drifting clouds of white dust across paddocks
where sheep hid dirty fleeces amid dry grass
and random clumps of thistles raged against the world.
We rattled over grids and dipped down dry fords
where twists of trees slid down into gorge country.

Memory said there were falls, water hurtling,
flash and roar, spray drifting up through the gums
to wet eager faces, cliffs hurling echoes
back at yells. This day there were only pools,
stagnant above and below, rimmed with green scum,
echoes muffled in the dry rocks and parched trees
drowned by thirsty wind muttering in our ears
as it set the steel fence wires to hum and sing.

This was a dry year; the auspices were bad
and held true. The water sat in shrinking pools,
the wind whined through railings. Nothing to do
but make a joke, turn from the remembered edge
and go back by another way, dustily
past elms lanced by afternoon light, alien
among gums, back to hotels and broken sleep
and the slow return to new places, old thoughts.

She Washes Him

The nurse holds the white bowl like a gift.
The new widow takes it, lets it sit
warming hands for a while, there by the bed.

There by the bed roses in a vase
droop yellow on the table. Water
slops from the bowl as she puts it down.

She puts it down and knows she must look
at the bed where he has lain these weeks
and lies still. So still. She takes a cloth.

She takes cloth, soaks water from the bowl,
water warm as blood, cool as pity.
She holds the damp cloth and waits. She looks.

She looks at his grey face, white stubble,
mouth opened in an O of surprise.
She takes him by the wrist, lifts his arm,

lifts his arm lightly up and washes
soft old skin. He has not stiffened yet.
She washes it all away and smiles

and smiles as he cannot with his O,
his closed eyes. She washes him and smiles
at each distant, each familiar part.

Each familiar part is washed, is dried.
Years are oiled away. It is over.
No smile. She steps back. The nurse holds her.

Dust

Each day flakes away. Mote after mote
we lose our skins to the restless air.
Tiny flakes jitter unseen until
the sharp sun spotlights them in their dance.

The snake's miracle of sliding out,
of leaving behind a year of skin,
is not for us. No neat summary
nor glorying in our new bright scales

but the slow return of molecules
to the world from which we gathered them
as food, drink and each uncounted breath.
We wipe yesterday with a soft cloth.

Scenes from a Silent Film

      1.

This could be a dance, almost,
between him and his ladder
the way he swings and turns it
on their route towards the wall.

      2.

It looks like the sort of wall
ladders should be put against.
It's wide and tall, featureless,
for going over, not through.

      3.

Now the almost-dance has stopped
there is brute force and huffing
will he won't he lifting up
slamming of ladder on wall.

      4.

Rituals precede a climb:
the flexing, spitting on hands
the cautious testing of rungs
and then a pratfall, for luck.

5.

A theatre of climbing
two steps up then one down
—unseen snakes of the ladder—
until he reaches the top.

6.

Theatre now of looking
into an unseen distance
down to an unseen ground
then up to a silent sky.

7.

The first and only close-up
shows a single expression:
one eyebrow raised in surprise
the other low and puzzled.

8.

All that is left is falling
both man and ladder as one
until his last moment flip
to land on his feet.

Gut Feeling

The body knows. It twists and clenches,
curls and twitches and grinds it.
The body knows but it will not tell
and we have not learned to ask.

This is what augurs tried to seize,
embalmers wished to preserve:
hairs on the neck and gooseflesh
and butterflies in the gut.

Here words, there images do nothing
that a tiny breath cannot.
We wait for a translator to tell
how flesh talks, what body knows.

Kafka at Work

Each day they are sent to us: instances
of pain, worked examples of life pressing
unbearably down, noted in due form
submitted for judgement.

By design every story is stripped back
to a wall of facts, rough and unplastered;
what cannot be diagnosed by doctors
must not and will not count.

This is what we ask of everyone
who makes a claim on us: describe the instant
when a life changed, describe without feeling
and without adjectives

that lyric moment, then send it to us.
Each day these moments come and we must look
must sift and scrutinise these shapes of fact
and judge their consequence.

But that is not enough. The law demands
that we explain ourselves and what we've done.
There is no form that this can take but prose:
our essay in response.

Official Greetings

The cards sidle in singly,
in pairs – restrained, official
bonhomie in approved form
the clean and careful noting
of a generic season.

See here a star, any star
and here a fir tree reduced
to lines and coloured angles.
This latest shows a landscape
unpeopled, temperate.

There is the pile for sending,
flat and arid as the rest
designed to avoid offence.
Now hand and pen vacillate
over a personal touch.

Plato as World Traveller

This city too is the one city. This room
in this hotel anchors itself in the same
room in every one of a hundred cities
that are the one city. Outside, the same cars
brawl in the same streets and pigeons startle,
scatter across a hundred skies that are one.
The planes that travel to this city and leave
for the next or return to their origin
link the one city to itself. Such order
moves towards the perfection where we all know
our places in the one place.
                                        It is poets
who ruin this: with distinctions, with stories
that find local habitations, local names
for people and for things; with old lies
that let each pigeon take its own arc of flight,
let each driver make the choices that lead home
or to gratitude in a stolen embrace
or even to screeching metal and to pain,
perhaps to death. The poets ruin order,
play dice with everything. Now they have trapped me
with freedom: I watch that young man bleed to death
in mangled metal, watch two lovers huddle
in shocked love. I watch and know that I have lost
my one city without ever gaining theirs.

The Idea of Busan

I might start by telling you this is a city
trying to become something else, something that clouds
fail to express in shuffling past sultry mountains,
something that lurks in the mountains under shadows
of huddled pines that wait for the axe and chainsaw.
You might not hear me over the roar of traffic,
the ratcheting of cicadas and the hot wind
sandpapering your ears, for this is a city
whose inarticulate shouts distract from thought.
We could walk, then, seaward to the sickled curve,
the sharp edge of sand that whets itself on the waves
while single-minded jet-skis go buffeting south.
The thought itself may hide past the rocks and headland,
in the rumble and clang of cranes, straining cables
and looming tons of metal edging into port.
We could follow it through the fat and slanting rain
that blows from a typhoon's edge up towards the hills
where a fortress has crumbled for two hundred years.
We would stand in the crowded politeness of trains,
zigzag through intentness and jostling of streets,
walk beside urgent freeways, squeezed by the tall piles
of stacked-up flats and mirrored glass of office blocks.
Then I would take you to where the cable-car hums,
impatient as the rain clears, take you swaying up
through drifts of fog and moving air as warm as sweat
to where trees huddle over the tumbledown walls.
Up there is muteness of wind and water and birds,
the quiet of history and of a high place.
We might stand together with the city laid out
and lent precision by distance. We might look down

and see the thought take shape: the city inveigling
itself into green valleys, encircling mountains
with roads and houses, pressing at the barriers
that restrained the armed weight of a peninsula;
the mountains pushing back with green and history,
the sea nibbling with waves, surging with tides of trade;
caught in between, the citizens wait urbanely
for the something else to come. It is not ours
to take or even to describe. We should leave it there,
leave that high place without worship or dominion,
sway downwards to the crowds and the noise; we would look
to the horizon where the night and typhoon come.

A Guide to Bohemia

The wine is good here, plentiful and cheap.
They dance in the streets as though making love,
slowly through a long night, or fast as blood
streaming from a knife-wound. Faces are pale
or livid; no-one seems to eat enough.
Poets loiter everywhere, wan, ignored
and no birds sing. White handkerchiefs
suppress endemic coughs, absorb the red
arterial blood. Antibiotics
are unavailable. Bring a supply.
Best accommodation is the garrets
if you don't mind sharing them with strangers.
You can get most things in exchange for sex
but be advised that love is never free.
Though it's distant, and sometimes fictional,
we recommend a visit to the coast.

A Mind of Winter

You can fall asleep in summer and wake to winter
to the bright weight of white pressing on evergreen boughs
and wind sifting soft flakes until everything is snow.

You can ease through afternoon as though you've sidestepped time
as the slush underfoot thickens and turns back to ice
and the early night suppresses the last of the day's glitter.

Insistent cold and growing dark leave no space to think
beyond the next step and the next through all-present wind
across paths of other hunched walkers moving like leaves

in an eddy of wind. Down the slope an edge of land
is bonded to the river with ice hardened by wind.
Night strips all warmth out and fixes everything in place:

water and land, ice underfoot and wind, drifted snow.
You walk into night and see what no one else beholds:
the obverse of winter, a world away, where sunlight is.

Near the Maelstrom

Towards midnight, the sun, slow as the last guest
at a solstice party, slips with a green flash
over the soft edge of the tabletop sea.
The boat rocks uneasily, not knowing how
to choose between the embrace of twilight
and the message the breeze carries direct
from the northern ice. Low islets shimmer;
the mainland coast holds out resolutely
between mountains and the insistent sea.
A bird dives, disappears. A log seesaws
in the even swell as it drifts southward.
Among the islands the water is held
in a rough bowl, shivering a little
as though cold, or nervous. From this unbalance
the bird flurries upward through the calm, a fish
twitching in its beak. One flick and swallow
are tonight's reply to daily hunger;
tomorrow is not yet here to ask the same
gnawing question. The log drifts, implacable
and straight towards the south where the sun,
insomniac, will soon begin its climb
back into light that refuses to fade.
The boat heads north to where the sun will not set;
a long wake bisects the horizon.

After Returning

Coming back was the hardest thing—
not the leaving or the journey—
coming back to known smiles, habits
as predictable as moonrise.

A story can only be told
a few times before it grows stale
Friends brush tellings away like crumbs
until space is cleared for silence.

The road is black under the moon.
Feet could walk down it, feet should dance
through puddles and will carry with them
old bones, as dawn brightens behind.

In the Wilderness

> *If there were water we should stop and drink*
> *Amongst the rock one cannot stop or think*
> *Sweat is dry and feet are in the sand*
> *If there were only water amongst the rock*
>
> T.S. *Eliot* The Waste Land

Back when I wore goatskins, the wells were few
but certain. I killed the man
I had called brother when he laughed at the stink
of my half-cured goatskins, at my rejected
sacrifice. The greasy smoke hugged the ground.
It has all changed now. Come here to the brink:
if there were water we should stop and drink

but there is not and has not been for years.
Imagine a month's fall of crushing rain
the wind and waves, feel the boat rise and sink
and hear the panic of confined animals.
In the end the waters fell and I fell
on rocks. The animals stampeded to the brink
—*amongst the rock one cannot stop or think*—

until all that was left was mud, drying,
prints of vanished stock. Memory
shrivels and dries into desert. If you stand
beside me now, you can see the bleached wood
on the top of this hill. That was our boat,
in this desert where salt forms on the hand,
sweat is dry and feet are in the sand.

I struck that rock over there with my staff
and water flowed for everyone to drink.
Smoke by day and fire by night is the clock
that marks my time and there is no water
now to quench it. There is no water and now
I thirst: the ground trembles in aftershock.
If there were only water amongst the rock.

The Feast of Valentine

Today was the festival of the wolf,
whose stalking and rending is forgotten,
who stared at paradise with yellow eyes.
Today is the day we exchange hearts
of flattened paper bought cheap from elsewhere.
There is no blood. Teeth are no longer sharp.

What big teeth they once were, as curved, as sharp
as the blade that sacrificed child to wolf
while his clear blue eyes were looking elsewhere.
Blood puddled on stone. We have forgotten
the price of safety, forgotten how hearts
were torn from warm flesh as light drained from eyes.

See where a young girl with the same blue eyes
walks the wild path. A hidden knife is sharp
in her basket. It is not enough. Hearts
can falter even before the grey wolf
lopes from the wood. She has forgotten
all that she was told. Her mind is elsewhere.

All the things we need to see are elsewhere,
hidden around the corners of our eyes.
Is there something we have not forgotten?
The scissors that slice red paper are sharp.
As I cut I could whistle like a wolf,
making what cannot be bought: conjoined hearts.

Once there were twin brothers with killers' hearts
left to die in the desert of elsewhere.
What does it mean to be mothered by a wolf,
to see some sort of love in yellow eyes?
No matter. They grew and in one sharp
burst of anger all love was forgotten.

There is so much that we have forgotten
or buried in the place we call our hearts.
Our vagueness takes the edge from all things sharp;
our tame love has lost the map to elsewhere
and bright sunlight hides the moon from our eyes,
but the shepherds' god always was a wolf.

Watch in moonlight for the wolf, forgotten
in open eyes, absent from bloodless hearts.
Wildness still lurks elsewhere. Its teeth are sharp.

Labyrinth

It stinks down here like cages in a zoo.
Water drops green from ceilings carved of rock
where thought condenses cold as mist on skin
that chafes against the gritty limestone walls.
This place is where things must be found again
that were lost in the moments between nightmare
and waking. The body remembers first:
thumping heart, shallow breath, muscles held tense
against the unknown. You clutch the thread
that slides and disappears around a curve.
Somewhere back there one waits, someone whose face
you no longer recall. You must go forward
through angled passages and crossing ways
where walls hide shadows shaped like horns.

No Looking Back

The story says you tripped before you called out
but you did not. No stumble, no slip or fall
as we struggled up a thousand slimy steps.
We climbed until cramp
locked our calves and our thighs trembled with strain.
Only breath was real, elbowing into lungs
then squeezing out. Sweat scraped at our eyes and dripped
down onto stone. Always I led, as ordered,
your shadow two plodding steps below, behind.
I did not look back and you never stumbled
nor did you cry out until the very end.
Sunlight on dry steps warmed the stone.
Morning held its welcomes of breeze and birdsong
when at last you called my name, shouted so loud
it bounced from wall to wall. It was then I looked
and you fell, you faded; you smiled.

A Hundred Times

This game anyone can play: take a word
that stands for something real—say chair, or key
—take and repeat that word a hundred times
until sense is driven out. Sound remains,
empty as a shirt dangling on the line,
but the chair seems gone, the key finds no lock.
You understand? An easy game. Let's begin.

Knock on Wood

The hungry ones whisper outside. They wait
for invitations that never come, gifts
that are rarely given. They wait as dark
smothers the last of day and the children
come knocking with games they don't understand.
The dead walk, even though their graves are closed,
and the children walk with them, unaware.
They want what we have, the hungry ones: warmth
held tight in blood, the life exhaled in breath.
Inside we touch and eat, we laugh and talk
of what may come, of half-expected things
that hope may bring and then we knock on wood
softly, with a joke. We should knock, harder,
unless we want the hungry ones to hear,
knock hard like the children now at the door
who proffer threats and ask for gifts.

Afterword

Some final thoughts, partly by way of disavowal. My hands may not be clean, but a chance to wash them is always welcome.

The poems in this collection were written over a number of years, normally in snatches of time stolen from the daily business of earning a living. Partly for that reason, the main impulse driving each of them was lyric and of the present. The voice that speaks belongs, largely and somewhat unfashionably, to the poet.

Each poem developed as a thing in itself, without an eye to any broader themes or unifying principles. As becomes clear when the individual poems are brought together, though, certain small but hardy obsessions do persist, despite best attempts to exorcise them.

The main obsession was, and remains, with that moment when we know beyond doubt that something significant has changed, but we are not yet sure exactly what it is. For me, that is the lyric moment —and one that should stand alone, without further explanation.

No broader narrative is intended, then, although the reader may find one—or several. She is entitled to do so. All suggestions will be gratefully received, particularly those that offer insight into the denouement.

More importantly, countless thanks are due to Suzanne Edgar, Melinda Smith and Michael Thorley. They saw the earliest versions of each of these poems. Through their tactful but rigorous comments they helped to turn inchoate drafts into finished products. Any remaining deficiencies are there despite their help.

Acknowledgments

Versions of some of the poems in this collection have previously appeared in *Australian Poetry Journal, the Canberra Times, foam:e* and the *Poetryetc Anthology*.

2018 Editions

The Uncommon Feast **Eileen Chong**
Inlandia **K A Nelson**
Peripheral Vision **Martin Dolan**
Ley Lines and Rustling Cedars **Niloofar Fanaiyan**
The Love of the Sun **Matt Hetherington**
Moving Targets **Jen Webb**
Things I Have Thought to Tell You Since I Saw You Last **Penelope Layland**
The Many Uses of Mint **Ravi Shankar**
Abstractions **Various**

2017 Editions

A Song, the World to Come **Miranda Lello**
Cities: Ten Poets, Ten Cities **Various**
The Bulmer Murder **Paul Munden**
Dew and Broken Glass **Penny Drysdale**
Members Only **Melinda Smith** and **Caren Florance**
the future, un-imagine **Angela Gardner** and **Caren Florance**
Proof **Maggie Shapley**
Black Tulips **Moya Pacey**
Soap **Charlotte Guest**
Isolator **Monica Carroll**
Ikaros **Paul Hetherington**
Work & Play **Owen Bullock**

all titles available from
www.recentworkpress.com

www.ingramcontent.com/pod-product-compliance
Lightning Source LLC
Chambersburg PA
CBHW030458010526
44118CB00011B/994